in case of emergency press

We are proud to acknowledge the Traditional Owners of country throughout Australia and to recognise their continuing connection to land, waters, and culture.

We pay our respects to their Elders.

We support recognition, reconciliation, and reparation.

Toward the Real

Poems for a New Reality

Angelo J. Letizia

in case of emergency press
http://www.icoe.com.au
Travancore, Victoria
Australia

Published by **in case of emergency press** 2022

Copyright © Angelo J. Letizia 2022

All rights reserved. Without limiting the rights under copyright reserved above, no part of this publication may be reproduced, stored in or introduced into a database and retrieval system or transmitted in any form or any means (electronic, mechanical, photocopying, recording or otherwise) without the prior written permission of both the owner of copyright and the above publishers.

ISBN 978-0-6453751-5-2

There is only poetry
And universes under her fingernails
Which she files away

from 'Is the earth here?'

Dedicated to Cici, my budding poet.

Table of contents

Preface	v
Where did we go wrong?	**1**
How will they know...	2
I am too tired...	3
Office buildings like a...	4
Open spaces...	5
Lewes	**6**
Braid the inches...	7
The concrete outside is an ovary...	8
Sludge in the pipes...	9
Is the earth here?	10
The 10,000 things settle on the rug...	11
Some things are beautiful...	12
We take the fraction...	13
Autumnal beings...	14
A country gestates...	15
I wish I could create worlds...	16
There is a terror in everyday things...	17
I am afraid that...	18
A jelly sky...	19
Place the marker in the ground...	20
Harvest the root...	21
Sow the algorithm into the tongue...	22
The lonely girl...	23
Vodka and water...	24
Office buildings made of raisins...	25
It will only be paradoxical for a short time...	26
How many shovels...	27
What do you know of October...	28
The salt in your voice	**29**
My wife boils yellow pears...	30
There are foetuses in traffic lights and bricks...	31
Come and leave this behind...	32
There are machinations in the sun...	33
A childless women waters...	34

You don't like my poetry...	36
No one cares about...	37
Can you regret the moon?	38
All is symbol now...	39
Can you requisition the sun?	41
I don't know how much time is left...	42
Growing up Catholic (the things I think)	**43**
Witness the posture...	44
We need purpose...	45
There is so much purpose here...	46
I have decided to rename the universe...	47
Here is your comedian	**48**
Spine	**49**
Blessed Deviance	**50**
The Spectacle	**53**
Chasm	**55**
Memory is a well-constructed house	**56**
Jesus walked through a...	57
The right words...	58
About the Author	**59**

Toward the Real

Poems for a New Reality

Angelo J. Letizia

Preface

Over the last few decades many theorists from many different fields and disciplines have tried to describe the changes taking place in society. Whatever we call it, a palpable change seems to be occurring. What this change boils down to, I think, is the desire for truth. What is real? How can one know? These are questions that drive us, thrill us, and terrify us. How can one truly know what is real? What if we cannot find or know the truth? What if we actually create truth? The poems in this book do not directly answer these questions. However, I think the poems themselves might be something close to an answer. But the poems are not intelligible answers, at least not to our modern scientific and linguistic systems. Truth may have evolved past these systems and now we need poetry to find truth.

Angelo J. Letizia, PhD.
Manchester, Maryland
23rd June, 2022

Where did we go wrong?

Canonize a devil
To watch him win
Canonize an algorithm
So it can sin
Just for you
There is so much you assume
And so much you don't know
Like how the plague drops slowly
Breaks into
Iridescent filaments
And plastic thrones
The markers of some wayward progress
Hidden in trunks of dead trees and telephone poles
Where did we go wrong?

How will they know
if it is ending?
Will borders surface
In the shoulder of some old desert road?
Will there be grotesque prophecies which
Enclose a desperate sky?
Pestilence and guillotines
Will leach an echo from the sun
And ascend
On a frosty morning
There is no harbor
No halfway point
We are already here

Toward the Real   Angelo J. Letizia

I am too tired
To take the garbage out
So let it stand like a monument
To my obsolescence
I yelled at my wife again
And the faucet is leaking
I cannot fix it
There are so many things
I do not know
Plumbing and carpentry
I want to become an
Antartican citizen
Deep south
Establish a colony in the ice
See the dark beautiful death
See it at night
As its creeps closer
Over the barren land
Finally
So I can sleep

Office buildings like a
Cancerous geometry
Dissect the sphere
Quiet voices
Drain the gas
From the sun
To reveal its bony husk
The currency for this life and the next
Every star is a door
Pour gas into them too
Fill the universe with fuel
To drown the husk
And start a new utopia

Open spaces
Pour like concrete
Or churches to fill
Underground pipes
Think with psalms and dirt
Streets become pipes
Streets become electric wires
And concrete again
But empty space
Is a beautiful geometry
An antidote
Among the debris
And obsolescence of your progress

Lewes

I am the memory
Shipwrecked
Strewn with glass
That you forget

I am the symbol
Which lies fallow
For 22 autumns
In the forest

The house has a crooked frame
But its angles are divine
Water drains on boards
And nourishes all ecosystems in the holy dirt below

The forest of memory
And stone
Is the architecture of your experience
You carry with you

Braid the inches
Into a voice
To surface the solstice
Rotate the frequency
And divide the labour
You have buried the borders
Flattened all of the origins
There are bells and divorces
And inscriptions
Lick the axiology
So you can breathe

The concrete outside is an ovary
A brittle birth tube
Built unknowingly by state workers
The salt and dust of the road
Is a placenta of sorts
Each car precedes the birth, brings us closer
Empty streets gestate
Outside the unsuspecting houses
Something is waiting to be born
It is almost here

Sludge in the pipes
May be divine
The universe squeezes through a tube
Mountains ground into a boiled paste
Sticks to a pan

The terror of everyday things
Rings in a phone
Chips, transistors in my hand
Bent toward the sun
It is the fear, the agony
And indifference
As I buy coffee
And have the septic pumped

There are so many businesses
To make your life easier
Landscaping and septic pumps
Oil and garage doors
Exterminators
All of these occupations are temporary though

Is the earth here?
Or is there only an image
Which we believe to be true
And solid
Maybe Berkeley was right
The rug is a dream
As is your success
There is only poetry
And universes under her fingernails
Which she files away

The 10,000 things settle on the rug
Piles of junk and plastic
Strewn on some
Abandoned kitchen floor
A rusted fork
And an empty laundry detergent bottle
Tyre jacks and pavement
Grease and notebooks
Double as some sort of soul
Or shadow
Which follows you
It's all there
All the time
Rivers of couches
And glass
Can be soothing
And fill the spaces
Left by shifting a foundation

Some things are beautiful
Right before they die
Full of colour
And light
Some things are ugly
And take time to die
But they do not know they are dying
They need advertisements
And heroes
To show them how

We take the fraction
To be the whole
Only because
It is refracted
Through what we know
And our experience
Through the corners
And gasoline
Through the landfills
Only to arrive
At the entrance
Of clarity and despair
A place of mirrors
And they hang
Like a dead branch
In the winter sun
Which has grown tired
But still shines
On the cold earth
Which will die soon

Autumnal beings
Slumber under the wood
They turn their blood to smoke
And give up the secret
Of their sclerosis
And wait
As they try to grow
A new solar system
In a beer can
On the side of the road
Grow a new world
With new logic
Let the old one die
So the autumnal beings
Can finally be happy

A country gestates
In the algorithms
And in the frothy wavelengths
Melodies of acquiescence
Ring dull
When stone and star
Form the barrier
Of this new sterile land
As it flickers
In the hollow of the skull

I wish I could create worlds
Maybe in the corner of my living room
In between the carpet fibres
Construct a utopia
With lines and angles
Blank space
Laid out in front of me
Like a pasture
In an old painting
Before there was television

There is a terror in everyday things
In concrete
And the washing machine
But still
I have to take out the trash
And drive to work

I am afraid that
the shape of the tree
Will separate from the leaves
And the trunk
And the raw stuff of the tree
Will overwhelm me without a shape
Without a form
Which is now brittle and useless
Like a cicada shell

A jelly sky
Spreads blue
Like a foundation of wax
To hold a new heaven
But this foundation
Eventually drains
To the earth
A puddle of wax and sky and dirt
Can no longer nourish
The fools
But they never deserved it anyway

Place the marker in the ground
Where the algorithm is buried
And where are the human voices in the forest?
Can any of this be reconciled?
Can the prophets atone for their mistakes?
Not if we break the arches
That support all their beliefs
A translucent Pentecost
Flowers in the asphalt
Gives birth
To the pataphysics
Which you now call home
Something different
Something paradoxical
But beautiful

Harvest the root
And apple seed
Harvest the bone
And the gasoline
Sow the end
And reap the beginning
Sow the rows with the garbage
Of this universe
Sow it with dead stars
And burnt out microprocessors
Bury the broken glass
Deep in the earth
Bury the old carpets
And washing machines
Harvest the utopia
Of peach pits
To live with
It's the best you can hope for now

Sow the algorithm into the tongue
Reap it
In the rectum
The algorithm is pitiless
And wired into open jaws
And who is left, when it is done?
The lonely men
The fragments and the imaginary numbers
The exponents?
There is only sand and glass
And pavement
Dust and fillings
Peach pit foundations
With rafters of cicada shells
Algorithms will make paste of us all

The lonely girl
With black hair and
A mask
Sits in the back of the old classroom
I wonder what she is thinking

Vodka and water
Gasoline and stars
Bleach in earth's core
And ammonia in the heart
But the ghosts are silent
Hammering in the grass
Asbestos souls
Hold together
All things you love

Office buildings made of raisins
Flags turn to kerosene
Draped on oak streets
Tyres transform into ideas
The unseen, the un-thought
Become streams of images
Which wash the logics dry
And brittle
Corners can no longer join
Anything we once loved
But we realized
That they were not needed
In the first place

It will only be paradoxical for a short time
The hierarchy is temporary
The swollen algorithms
Will not last long
It's almost time for them to burst
And shrivel

How many shovels
have you accrued?
How many cycles
Have deposited you here
To translate the furniture
And decipher the absence?
But your vanity yokes you to the blaze
So you cannot evolve any further
And your heart
Becomes a fossil

What do you know of October
And its leaves?
All you know
Are bald used up tyres
And clean floors
The vestigial forms of your memories
Are buried in October
They can liberate you
But you still sacrifice them
to some fictitious god you claim to love

The salt in your voice

Did you brush your teeth after?
Watch TV?
Where were your feet? On the bed, the floor?
What did your friends say? Did you even tell them?
Did you eat breakfast the next day?
Did the bacon remind of you of your freedom?
I wonder if it all nourished you
And if it was worth it?
But how can I judge?
And why do I care?

Like an obsolete TV
You flicker when you walk
Disability is rust, mould and blight.
And you won't be fixed. Ever.
But the lesions cannot erase those deeds
Nor the salt in your voice
But those deeds
Like dead stars
Still shine their light across the universe
Perhaps memory
Is also a disability

My wife boils yellow pears
In cinnamon milk
The house smells sweet
I prepare the whipped cream
And coffee
Outside, the red and golden leaves
Come to rest on the earth
Waiting to decay, waiting to sleep
Because it is October again
The month of beauty
And the month of ashes
But my wife still sets the table
And I set the napkins

There are foetuses in traffic lights and bricks
Gestating
Waiting their turn to be born
And to leave the husks behind

Broken glass, sunflower seeds and orange rinds are placentas
They are comforting in a way
The same way a landfill is
There is a peace in these things
In these scraps we take for granted
Afterbirth of the ages

Come and leave this behind
Leave the asphalt vegetation
Leave the temperature
Ignore the neon foetuses
Those gaseous creatures
In forgotten bulbs
Forget the magnitude and velocity
Let the bananas decay
All this is some sort of celestial index
A classification scheme of dead stars and dwarf planets
The phylum of dental crowns
That line the junkyards
Leave all this
To a devil

There are machinations in the sun
Little rooms with vacuums
Factories that make blood
And paper and stars
How many revolutions are there in the ice?
On Pluto or in the dark
Matter or the universe you never see

Are there heroes in the core of Eris?
Archetypes in the Andromeda?
You have built houses that no one uses
Carpeted foundations in earth's mantle
But we live on the crust
Trust the topsoil, trust the clay
Where no seeds grow
The dumpster is a throne
Milk cartons and plastic spoons
Are divine, oracles of a sort
They are the stilted future
The aborted tongues of what comes next and forever

A childless women waters
Her garden she has
A college degree which she
Thinks is worthless
And
Grey hair and a new car
She sits on a deck on a
Sunday
In some spring
She will forget
Her laundry sways
Peacefully
In the April sun
She sits on the deck, she may be lonely, may
Be content
The hills and flowers grow around
Her
The rusted screen door
She can keep open now
Is no gateway or portal
Just an entrance to the living room
With a thousand figurines
And fake flowers
Her air conditioner works again
And her little cottage could sell
For a quarter million
But she would never leave

This is her universe
Her lonely universe
With vinyl siding
How many citizens are like this?
How many beings in spring, with old flowers
But no new galaxies?

You don't like my poetry
Because I don't write about
Sucking a bird's dick
My poetry isn't detailed enough
And I don't write about politics
What you consider art
Is the standard
The ivory tower
But my poems are barbed wire
And landmines
Little hammers and moles
It might be a day
A year
A century
Your success is a simulacrum

No one cares about
The numbers between 1 and 2
No one cares about
The things I do
Or the devils in the pavement
Or the rooms in the sun
No one notices
The sticky garbage
That floats by the corner
No one cares about
The edges or
Abandoned slaughterhouses
There are too many bricks
And too many fractions
No one cares about
A disassembled shoe and universes between the laces
No one cares about
The things I do

Can you regret the moon?
That round tumour
Metastasizing in the sky?

Can you regret the sun?
Even after it burns to a husk
Because the sun is not a star
It is an imposter
There is no fuel
Just a grisly infrastructure
Bones in the cornea

Can you regret the black holes and microbes?
The crowned teeth, the fossils and sediments
Underneath the crust?

I have found a way to regret it all,
To regret the seen and the unseen
To regret the Anthropocene

All is symbol now
With multiple meanings
A door is an entrance, gateway and exit
To something better
While always being
A wooden door
In the universe of symbols and stars
Meanings accumulate like dust
Like rugs
And old paint cans
In the garage
A hand splits a tree
Between wood and life
Between growth and lumber
Now

Foliage breaks on a cylinder
As the street signs are lost
Red suitcases and notebooks
Become the cause
Of some revolution, somewhere
Of some embryo in the corner
Geologic time moves slow here
In these corners
It plods, quietly, enormously
Like an ancient predator
Like a migration of birds

Who don't know they are symbols
Flying in forms of blood and feathers and
Spreading meanings to modern peasants
Who ignore infinity

Can you requisition the sun?
Return the guillotine
Pack up the plague
There are receipts for these things
Scattered in parking lots
Dumpsters double as filing cabinets
Invoices scratched in tin foil
That fill the bureaucracy
Like water, or oil, or plasma
Monotonous scripts
Mouthing in aging phones
These offices grow in moonlight
In an old field
On the side of some desolate highway

I don't know how much time is left
But the scrap metal is hungry
The sky yawns impatiently
There is not much left to do
Aging wood becomes a consciousness now
It lets us know what we could have become
There is an old pumpkin under the porch
Which rots into a god
The clocks have stopped ticking
And the universe has grown a little colder
It won't be long now

Growing up Catholic (the things I think)

I wonder if
The woman leaning over
The skinless chicken thighs
In the produce section
Has a sex drive
Her purse strap
Is positioned innocently,
Yet seductively, between her breasts
And her tennis shoes
Squeak next to the lobster tank
She debates between chicken packages
To feed her family
(She has a wedding ring on)
Did she have sex last night? Did she give head?
Her yoga pants
Wrap tight around her butt
Like a crescent moon
Beaming over the linoleum

Witness the posture
The ultraviolet collapse
Which suggests the frequency
There is a realization here
But you must labour to find it
A buried axiology
Which discriminates
Which spawns a horizon
And a vacuum
For you to love comfortably
A space where all morals are equal
And arbitrary
Where epistemology is
Botulism
In broken cans
Disciplines span the gravel
And I sympathize with them
And their purple blood
Not of one world or the other

We need purpose
Like genocides
Or a house in the woods
By a lake
Where little caterpillars crawl
On leaves in the cool shade
There is nihilism here
And broken glass
On a hardwood floor
But the floor is an imposter
And the trees laugh outside

There is so much purpose here
In the corners and the spackle
On the lined paper
There is a purpose in the mottled tin roof of the church
And the unsubstantiated opinion
The blue metallic siding is meaningful
In an industrial way
You plant shrubs
Packed on the back of a trailer
There is grass here
And a question
Why do we need to think?
The professional thinkers ponder the shrubs
And the siding and leave us with more frustrating questions
They cannot communicate
So just plant the shrubs and fill the oil
Wait for the power tools to oxidize in an ecstasy of forgetting
So nothing can be built

I have decided to rename the universe
And all the things of the earth
I have grown tired of the present names
I want endless names
Like watery graves
Like black tar, formless and unforgiving

I will bring the stale syllables to the
Guillotine
In a silent procession
March each useless utterance to the scaffold
Let them ring one last time
Before they fall into the basket

I have grown tired of axiologies
And diagnoses
I have grown sick of accolades
And memories
Consign them all to the crematorium
I want them all to burn

I wonder what the world will look like with new names. Pity
I will not be able to tell you.

Here is your comedian

eggshell lip
cracked
and arranged into a grin
brain bag pumped
with serotonin
bolt the bones with steel rods
to support the smiling form
among the others
polish and push it around
ground its heart current
electrocute the melancholy mood
washing machine plugged into eye socket
wash it, bleach the frown
bleach skin
detergent and start again
rum and gin fuel the happy machine
laugh with colleagues
prop the bones in the carpet
stab the vacuum in the back
to abort the demons coiled on the spine
vacuum is jammed with blood
but I can be the king of this shindig
With a little help

Spine

Heart attack overweight
Chicken and grease congeal
In the stomach
And the back
Is old fences
Vertebrates have no grip
Slip out of sockets and chain link
Useless barricades but
Bandages wrapped tightly now
Colour of flesh
You don't notice them
Like King Tut walking
Through his gardens on sunny days
Under the skin
The flowers in his stomach
The fence in his back
Bloom and break all under the cloth
Rattle, shake
He is not king anymore
Just a mummy, a ghost
With my face

Blessed Deviance

Bone in circle
Soft ring
Tongue the secret
From the
Meaty flesh
Under
The cotton
Hot salt shot
All of this
Is a new
Sociology
Of the
Oesophagus

The next stop

He sees a friendless creature
Crawling
Through stones
And smooth buildings
Limping across
Unnoticed sidewalks
Whispering to itself
Shaking its dirty head
At invisible answers

They meet

The creature
Embraces the other
Dirt and blood
Can no longer be felt

"What is your name, friend?"

But the creature now stands motionless
Embracing
Erased
The face contorts
Straightens
The friendless body twists

And limps away
Because it is friendless

The creature is gone
And he is hungry

The Spectacle

The rope is thick
—but the will is stronger
Buildings taunt him
With outstretched arms
"we will serve the means"

It is tempting

Artificial lights
Maps, streetlights and store lights warm him
Light the pavement
A lighted path
To a graveyard
With a headstone
(made from the glass of a store window)
The ground covered in dirt
(collected from subway terminals)
The buildings whisper
"it could be yours"
The rope is thick
—but the will is weakening

Spectators gather in windows
—and laugh
(they thought they were innocent)
They watched the will suspend
Under the tension of a thick rope

The moonlight is reflected on
A hanging crucifix
And the rope breaks
This is not the end

Chasm

Cracks separate in the walls
Between windows
Span the ceiling
No one sees the universe drip
Into the subway
Stars planets and meteors
Swirl between these cracks
In the concrete wall
Dancing over the crusts of stale bread
Light years and galaxies
Expand in silent choruses at midnight
For me
Their prisoner
Even when the moss crawls in the mouth
I've been sick for weeks
Maybe I am dead?
Hopefully the astronaut skin will rip
Set the memories free to drift in space
Like dead planets
Sailing the universe
In solitude

Memory is a well-constructed house

Memory is a well-constructed house
With rafters of bone
Where
Ciphers haemorrhage in the windowsill
To mediate between an indifferent sensation
And a pitiless perception
That breaks on a wooden desk
In a rarely used room
Full of dust

Jesus walked through a
Trapdoor
In the moon
And sat in a booth
At a diner in Baltimore
Where he ordered a water and fries
And tipped the waitress generously
He walked past the bank
And the gun shop
And went to the park
Where he sat on a bench
And ignored the moms
Jesus doesn't give a fuck about your chicken sandwiches
He bought a beer and walked back to heaven
Without talking to anyone

The right words
Cannot describe
The wrong situation
Clawed fish die in the air
And birds drown
In the ocean
There is so much wrong here
The bookshelf
Has made itself
Unintelligible
A wooden hieroglyph
Geometric arrangement
Of the ineffable
I finally learned how to read it
The soft pears in the dirty fridge
Give up their secret
In the syrup scraped off the door
There is more in the paint and paper
In the double yellow line
And in the street sign
It's all there to be read
But the end might come sooner than we think
So it doesn't really matter

About the Author

Angelo J. Letizia is a professor of education at Notre Dame of Maryland University in Baltimore, Maryland.

In addition to *Toward the Real*, Angelo has published three books of poetry with Silver Bow Press, and numerous academic monographs, articles, and essays. He lives in the United States with his wife and three children.

www.ingramcontent.com/pod-product-compliance
Lightning Source LLC
Chambersburg PA
CBHW020329010526
44107CB00054B/2037